TEXAS LORE Volume Six

UNUSUAL STORIES FROM TEXAS' HISTORY

by Patrick M. Reynolds

Published by

The Red Rose Studio
Willow Street, PA 17584

To
my mother-in-law
Viola M. Gouldner

Copyright © 1988 by Patrick M. Reynolds
ISBN 0-932514-18-9

Printed In The U.S.A.

Contents

THE JUMANO INDIANS

WERE NOMADIC HUNTERS AND TRADERS WHO INHABITED SOUTH-WEST TEXAS ABOUT 300 YEARS AGO. SPANISH EXPEDITIONS OF THE EARLY 1600's VISITED THE JUMANOS ALONG THE CONCHO RIVER NEAR PRESENT SAN ANGELO. A LIVELY TRADE DEVELOPED BETWEEN THEM, ESPECIALLY IN DEER AND BISON HIDES.

THE JUMANOS WERE IMPORTANT TO TEXAS' HISTORY: CONSTANTLY ON THE MOVE, THEY HELPED SPREAD CULTURE AND IDEAS AMONG THE OTHER TRIBES.

ALSO, THEY BLOCKED THE LIPAN-APACHES FROM ADVANCING SOUTHWARD FOR ALMOST A CENTURY WHILE HELPING THE SPANIARDS EXPLORE TEXAS.

IT IS BELIEVED THAT AFTER 1771 THE JUMANOS WERE ABSORBED BY THE APACHES.

The Oldest Highway In North America,

KNOWN AS *EL CAMINO REAL*, SPANISH FOR *THE ROYAL ROAD*, WAS STARTED BY THE SPANISH CONQUISTADORES IN MEXICO AROUND 1519. THE TEXAS PORTION WAS BLAZED IN 1690 BY DOMINGO TERAN de los RIOS, FIRST SPANISH GOVERNOR OF TEXAS. AT THE TIME, MONCLOVA IN COAHUILA, MEXICO WAS THE PROVINCIAL CAPITAL OF TEXAS.

HIS ROUTE CONNECTED MONCLOVA TO THE SPANISH MISSIONS ACROSS EAST TEXAS THROUGH SAN ANTONIO AND NACOGDOCHES TO LOS ADAES NEAR PRESENT-DAY ROBELINE, LOUISIANA. LOS ADAES WAS THE CAPITAL OF TEXAS FROM 1721 TO 1773.

IN 1915 THE TEXAS LEGISLATURE APPROPRIATED $5,000 TO SURVEY AND MARK THE ROAD. TODAY IT IS STATE HIGHWAY 21 AND PART OF I-35.

THE COMANCHEROS

WERE TRADERS FROM THE NEW MEXICO AREA WHO DID BUSINESS WITH THE COMANCHES AND OTHER PLAINS INDIANS IN TEXAS. MOST OF THEIR TRADE WAS IN THE CANYONS AND SECONDARY PLAINS OF THE *LLANO ESTACADO*, A HIGH PLATEAU THAT STRETCHES FROM THE WEST-CENTRAL PART OF TEXAS TO THE PANHANDLE.

THE COMANCHEROS' TRADE BEGAN IN 1786 AND LASTED ABOUT A CENTURY. AFTER THE BUFFALO HERDS WERE KILLED AND THE INDIANS WERE CONFINED TO RESERVATIONS, THE BASIS FOR THE COMANCHEROS' WAY OF LIFE WAS SHATTERED.

The Fort Ramirez Legend

AROUND THE LATE 1700's OR EARLY 1800's, ANTONIO AND VICTORIANO RAMIREZ BUILT THE *RANCHO de los JABONCILLOS*, KNOWN AS FORT RAMIREZ, ON THE WEST BANK OF THE NUECES RIVER. SUPPOSEDLY THE FIRST STRUCTURE ERECTED IN LIVE OAK COUNTY, IT CONTAINED A TANYARD, CORRALS, AND RANCH HOUSES.

IN 1813 THE MEXICANS REVOLTED AGAINST THEIR SPANISH OVERLORDS AND THE FRONTIER TROOPS (PRESIDIALES) WERE WITHDRAWN. CONSEQUENTLY, THE INDIANS ATTACKED THE FEW SCATTERED RANCHEROS AND THE RAMIREZES LEFT IN A HURRY.

LEGEND HAS IT THAT THEY ESCAPED THROUGH A TUNNEL WHERE THEY STASHED THEIR MONEY & VALUABLES. TREASURE HUNTERS VIRTUALLY LEVELED FORT RAMIREZ LOOKING FOR THAT CACHE. NOBODY HAS EVER ADMITTED FINDING IT.

The Dream Capital of Texas

ALARMED BY THE INFLUX OF AMERICAN SETTLERS INTO TEXAS DURING THE 1820's, THE MEXICAN GOVERNMENT ERECTED A LINE OF FORTS TO KEEP OUT THE INTRUDERS. **TENOXTITLAN,** ANCIENT AZTEC MEANING *PRICKLY PEAR,* WAS THE FORT LOCATED 8 MILES FROM CALDWELL. ITS COMMANDANT HOPED IT WOULD BECOME THE CAPITAL OF TEXAS.

THE SETTLERS, HOWEVER, KEPT COMING AND, IN 1832, THE MEXICANS ABANDONED THE FORT.

SUBSEQUENTLY, THE "NEW" TEXANS USED THE FORT AS A SUPPLY CENTER AND MUSTERING POINT FOR EXPEDITIONS AGAINST HOSTILE INDIANS.

TENOXTITLAN WAS SUGGESTED AS THE CAPITAL OF THE TEXAS REPUBLIC, BUT AUSTIN WON OUT. THE FORT WAS FINALLY ABAN- DONED IN 1841.

Marauders & Mercury

THE WILD, RUGGED TERRAIN OF THE **BIG BEND** REGION WAS, FOR CENTURIES, A HUNTING GROUND FOR APACHE & COMANCHE WARRIORS, AND A HAVEN FOR OUTLAWS & SMUGGLERS.

RICH DEPOSITS OF MERCURY WERE DISCOVERED HERE ABOUT 1900, AND THE MINING TOWN OF **STUDY BUTTE** EVOLVED AROUND THE *BIG BEND CINNABAR MINE*. FORTY YEARS LATER THE MINE STARTED TO LOSE MONEY AND WAS CLOSED. A LATER ATTEMPT TO REESTABLISH PRODUCTION FAILED.

RIVER SHIPPING IN PIONEER TEXAS

WAS MAINLY ON THE BRAZOS, AND WASHINGTON-ON-THE-BRAZOS WAS AN IMPORTANT PORT AFTER THE FIRST STEAMER REACHED THERE IN 1840.

RIVER NAVIGATION WAS DIFFICULT ON MOST OF TEXAS' MEANDERING RIVERS BECAUSE THEY WERE TOO SHALLOW, OFTEN FLOODED, AND MANY WERE CLOGGED WITH DRIFTWOOD THAT HAD TO BE CLEARED.

DURING THE DAYS OF THE TEXAS REPUBLIC, SOME ENTREPRENEURS STARTED TO SHIP COTTON, HIDES, AND LUMBER FROM THE INTERIOR TO THE COAST ON THE COLORADO RIVER. ABOUT 15 MILES ABOVE ITS MOUTH, THEY ENCOUNTERED A JUMBLE OF TIMBERS—SOME FLOATING, SOME SUBMERGED—CHOKING OFF THE RIVER FOR A DISTANCE OF 3 TO 8 MILES. THIS OBSTACLE WAS KNOWN AS

the Colorado River "Raft."

IN SPITE OF THIS, THE KEEL-BOAT "DAVID CROCKETT" WAS THE FIRST BOAT TO NAVIGATE THE RIVER, IN 1838.

LATER, FLATBOATS BROUGHT PRODUCTS AS FAR AS THE "RAFT," WHERE THE GOODS WERE UN-LOADED AND HAULED BY WAGON TO MATAGORDA.

AFTER THE CIVIL WAR, RAILROADS FINALLY SOLVED TEXAS' FREIGHT-MOVING PROBLEMS.

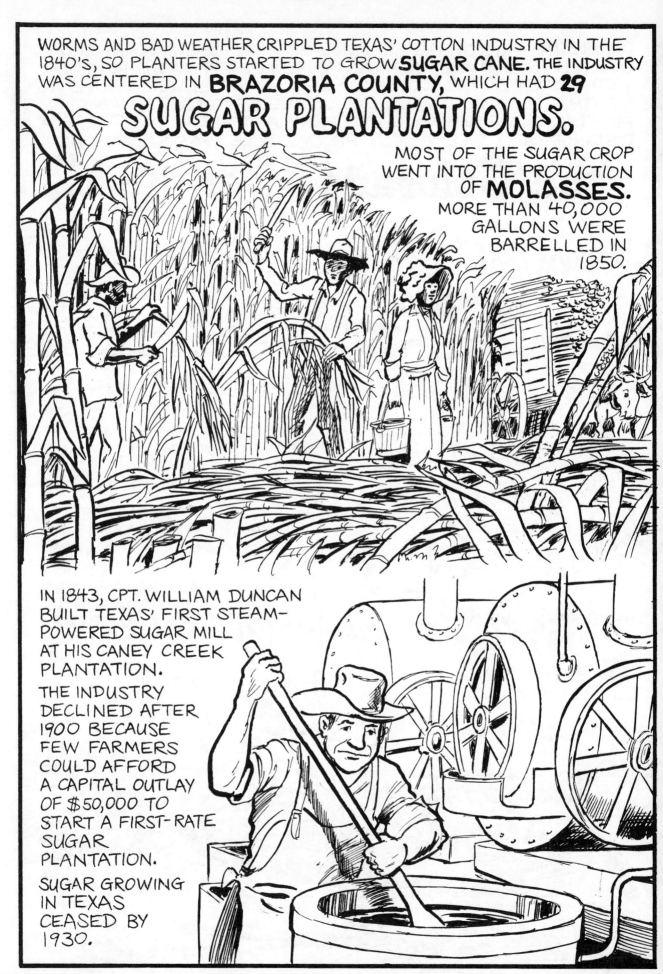

WORMS AND BAD WEATHER CRIPPLED TEXAS' COTTON INDUSTRY IN THE 1840's, SO PLANTERS STARTED TO GROW **SUGAR CANE.** THE INDUSTRY WAS CENTERED IN **BRAZORIA COUNTY,** WHICH HAD **29**

SUGAR PLANTATIONS.

MOST OF THE SUGAR CROP WENT INTO THE PRODUCTION OF **MOLASSES.** MORE THAN 40,000 GALLONS WERE BARRELLED IN 1850.

IN 1843, CPT. WILLIAM DUNCAN BUILT TEXAS' FIRST STEAM-POWERED SUGAR MILL AT HIS CANEY CREEK PLANTATION.

THE INDUSTRY DECLINED AFTER 1900 BECAUSE FEW FARMERS COULD AFFORD A CAPITAL OUTLAY OF $50,000 TO START A FIRST-RATE SUGAR PLANTATION.

SUGAR GROWING IN TEXAS CEASED BY 1930.

The Baptist Church In Texas

Z. N. MORRELL ORGANIZED A BAPTIST CHURCH IN WASHINGTON-ON-THE-BRAZOS IN 1837. NOAH T. BYARS, IN WHOSE BLACKSMITH SHOP TEXAS' DECLARATION OF INDEPENDENCE WAS SIGNED AND ADOPTED, WAS A CHARTER MEMBER OF THAT CHURCH.

MISSIONARIES INCLUDING JAMES HUCKINS AND RUFUS BURLESON HELPED ORGANIZE FIFTY CHURCHES ACROSS TEXAS INTO THE BAPTIST STATE CONVENTION IN 1848.

IN 1841, WITH LESS THAN 300 BAPTISTS IN ALL OF TEXAS, THE BAPTIST EDUCATION SOCIETY WAS FORMED. FROM THIS MEAGER BEGINNING SPRANG BAYLOR UNIVERSITY, HARDIN-SIMMONS UNIVERSITY, WAYLAND BAPTIST COLLEGE, AND OTHER FINE UNIVERSITIES.

TEXAS BAPTISTS BEGAN TO OPEN HOSPITALS IN 1903 WHEN BAYLOR HOSPITAL, DALLAS WAS FOUNDED. THE HOUSTON BAPTIST HOSPITAL OPENED IN 1907, FOLLOWED BY THE HILLCREST MEMORIAL SANITARIUM AT WACO AND THE HENDRIX MEMORIAL HOSPITAL IN ABILENE IN 1924.

GETTING CORNERED

THE NORTHEAST CORNER OF THE TEXAS PANHANDLE WAS ESTABLISHED BY LAW IN 1850 TO INTERSECT 100° LONGITUDE WITH 36°30' LATITUDE, 8½ MILES FROM FOLLETT, LIPSCOMB COUNTY. HOWEVER, TEXAS AND OKLAHOMA ARGUED OVER THE EXACT SPOT FOR OVER SEVENTY YEARS.

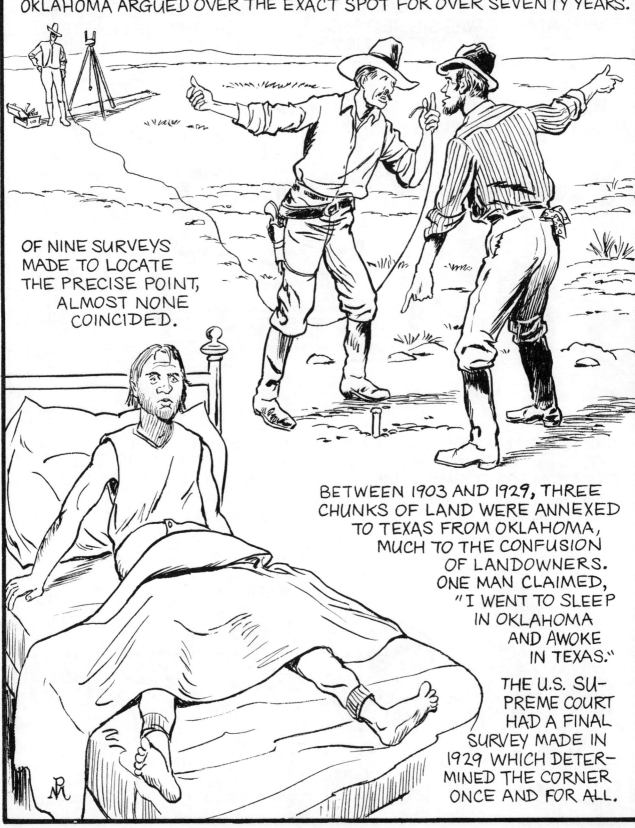

OF NINE SURVEYS MADE TO LOCATE THE PRECISE POINT, ALMOST NONE COINCIDED.

BETWEEN 1903 AND 1929, THREE CHUNKS OF LAND WERE ANNEXED TO TEXAS FROM OKLAHOMA, MUCH TO THE CONFUSION OF LANDOWNERS. ONE MAN CLAIMED, "I WENT TO SLEEP IN OKLAHOMA AND AWOKE IN TEXAS."

THE U.S. SUPREME COURT HAD A FINAL SURVEY MADE IN 1929 WHICH DETERMINED THE CORNER ONCE AND FOR ALL.

The Port Isabel Lighthouse

WAS BUILT IN 1852 BY THE U.S. TREASURY DEPT.

DURING THE CIVIL WAR, AS THE YANKEES WERE ABOUT TO OVERRUN THE LOWER RIO GRANDE VALLEY IN 1863, COL. "RIP" FORD OF THE TEXAS RANGERS STOLE THE LENS TO PREVENT THE ENEMY FROM USING IT TO GUIDE THEIR SHIPS.

CONSEQUENTLY, UNION SHIP CAPTAINS COULD NOT EASILY NAVIGATE AT NIGHT AND SOME OF THEM RAN AGROUND.

THE LIGHTHOUSE CEASED OPERATION IN 1905. IT IS NOW A STATE HISTORIC SHRINE & ONE OF THE SMALLEST STATE PARKS IN TEXAS.

THE LENS THAT FORD TOOK WAS NEVER FOUND.

The First Air-Conditioned House In Texas

WAS BUILT AROUND 1853 IN **SEGUIN** BY COL. JOSHUA **YOUNG** FOR HIS DAUGHTER. SINCE THE CRIMEAN WAR WAS GOING ON AT THE TIME, THE COLONEL CALLED THE PLACE **"SEBASTOPOL."**

THE ENTIRE ROOF WAS COVERED WITH A **TIN-LINED RESERVOIR** WHICH COOLED THE HOUSE AND PROVIDED A WATER SUPPLY DURING INDIAN RAIDS.

ALSO, AN UNDERGROUND **ESCAPE TUNNEL** LED FROM BENEATH THE HOUSE TO WALNUT CREEK ABOUT 100 YARDS AWAY.

THE SEGUIN CONSERVATION SOCIETY RESTORED THE HOUSE AND IT IS OPEN FOR VISITORS AT 704 W. ZORN ST.

The First Telegraph In Texas

WAS ESTABLISHED BY THE TEXAS & RED RIVER TELEGRAPH COMPANY IN **MARSHALL** ON FEB. 14, 1854. THE COMPANY OFFERED CONNECTIONS WITH NEW ORLEANS AND ALEXANDRIA, LA AND NATCHEZ, MS. LATER THAT YEAR THE LINE WAS EXTENDED TO HENDERSON, CROCKETT, RUSK, HOUSTON, AND GALVESTON.

WIRES WERE STRUNG FROM TREETOP TO TREETOP, AND OPERATORS CLOSED THEIR OFFICES TO REPAIR THE LINES.

BY 1870 THERE WAS AN ESTIMATED 1,500 MILES OF TELEGRAPH WIRE IN TEXAS.

ON FEB. 9, 1972 THE FIRST TELEGRAPH OFFICE IN TEXAS WAS CLOSED.

IN 1854, SECRETARY OF WAR JEF-FERSON DAVIS ORDERED A FORT TO BE BUILT IN THE VAST OPEN REGION OF WEST TEXAS TO PROVIDE WATER AND PROTECT GOLD SEEKERS AND SETTLERS HEADING FOR CALIFORNIA.

GENERAL PERSIFOR F. SMITH SELECTED A SITE IN A BOX CAN-YON NEAR LIMPIA CREEK IN THE DAVIS MOUNTAINS, AND CALLED IT

FORT DAVIS.

SIX COMPANIES OF THE 8th U.S. INFANTRY UNDER LT. COL. WASHINGTON SEAWELL HAD TO FIGHT HOSTILE INDIANS ON THEIR WAY TO THE SITE AND WHILE THEY WERE BUILDING THE FORT. SEAWELL HATED THIS LOCATION BECAUSE THE INDIANS COULD EASILY SNEAK UP AND ATTACK FORT DAVIS, WHICH THEY DID FOR THE NEXT SEVEN YEARS.

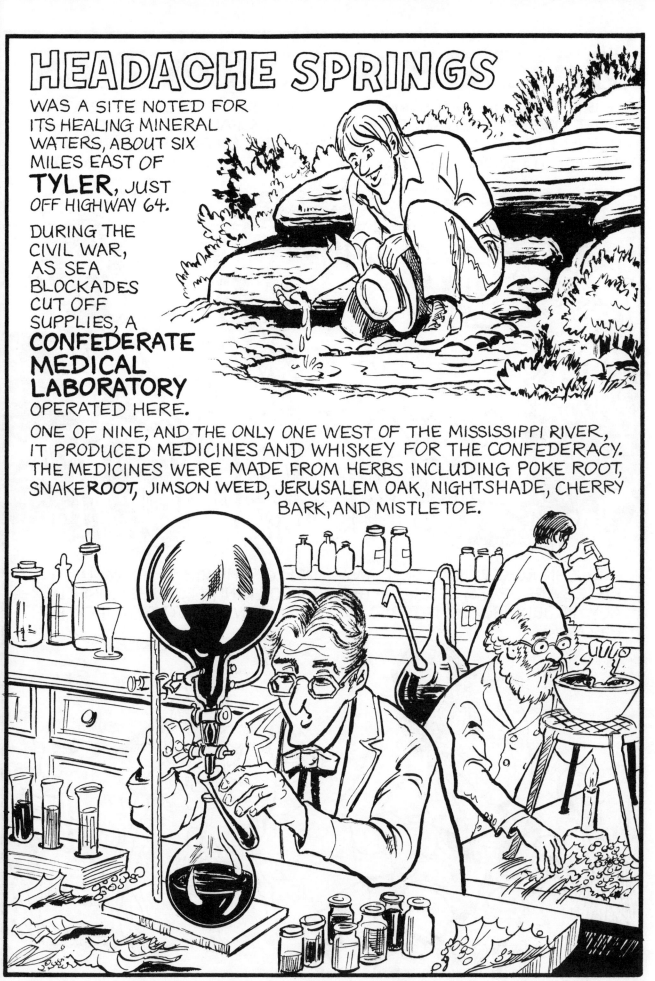

HEADACHE SPRINGS

WAS A SITE NOTED FOR ITS HEALING MINERAL WATERS, ABOUT SIX MILES EAST OF **TYLER**, JUST OFF HIGHWAY 64.

DURING THE CIVIL WAR, AS SEA BLOCKADES CUT OFF SUPPLIES, A **CONFEDERATE MEDICAL LABORATORY** OPERATED HERE.

ONE OF NINE, AND THE ONLY ONE WEST OF THE MISSISSIPPI RIVER, IT PRODUCED MEDICINES AND WHISKEY FOR THE CONFEDERACY. THE MEDICINES WERE MADE FROM HERBS INCLUDING POKE ROOT, SNAKE **ROOT**, JIMSON WEED, JERUSALEM OAK, NIGHTSHADE, CHERRY BARK, AND MISTLETOE.

BAYLOR'S MOUNTIES

WHEN THE CIVIL WAR STARTED IN APRIL, 1861, THE FEDERAL GOVERN-
MENT TRANSFERRED SOLDIERS FROM THEIR FAR WEST OUTPOSTS FOR
USE IN THE CRITICAL BATTLES IN THE EAST. SMALL, WEAKENED DE-
TACHMENTS WERE LEFT BEHIND TO SECURE THE WESTERN FRONTIER.

COL. JOHN ROBERT BAYLOR, COMMANDER OF THE 2nd TEXAS MOUNTED
RIFLES AT EL PASO, SENSED A GREAT OPPORTUNITY FOR THE CONFEDER-
ACY. IN JULY, 1861, HE LED 250 MEN INTO NEW MEXICO TO ATTACK FORT
FILLMORE.

THE FORT FILLMORE FIASCO

FORT FILLMORE, NEW MEXICO WAS MANNED BY 700 YANKEES IN JULY, 1861. AT THE APPROACH OF THE CONFEDERATES, THE 2nd TEXAS MOUNTED RIFLES UNDER COL. JOHN R. BAYLOR...

THE UNION COMMANDER PANICKED AND ORDERED THE EVACUATION OF THE FORT.

HIS STUPIDITY WAS COMPOUNDED BY THE ACTIONS OF HIS TROOPS WHO FILLED THEIR CANTEENS WITH WHISKEY INSTEAD OF WATER.

BY THE TIME THE HARD-RIDING TEXANS CAUGHT UP WITH THE FLEEING SOLDIERS, THE YANKEES WERE REDUCED TO A DRUNKEN RABBLE JUST DYING TO SURRENDER.

The Confederate "Territory of Arizona"

BY THE END OF 1861, COL. J.R. BAYLOR AND HIS TEXAS MOUNTIES OCCUPIED ALL OF THE UNION FORTS IN NEW MEXICO. HE CREATED THE CONFEDERATE "TERRITORY OF ARIZONA."

WITH THE YANKEES ON THE RUN, BAYLOR RODE WEST TO TUSCON AND TOOK CONTROL OF THE FEDERAL GARRISONS IN ARIZONA.

BAYLOR NAMED HIMSELF GOVERNOR, AND THE CONFEDERATE CONGRESS CONFIRMED HIS TITLE.

DECLARING MESILLA, NEW MEXICO AS HIS CAPITAL, BAYLOR ESTABLISHED A CONSTITUTIONAL GOVERNMENT IN WHICH ALL KEY POSTS WERE HELD BY TEXANS.

BAYLOR'S BRAINSTORM

COL. JOHN BAYLOR'S MAJOR HEADACHE AS THE CONFEDERATE GOVERNOR OF THE TERRITORY OF ARIZONA WAS THE MESCALERO APACHES. EVER SINCE THE NORTHERN FORCES EVACUATED, THESE INDIANS HAD BEEN RAIDING THE LOCAL RANCHES.

IN MARCH, 1862, BAYLOR GAVE AN UNUSUAL ORDER TO ONE OF HIS OFFICERS:

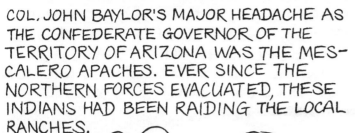

INVITE ALL THE INDIANS INTO YOUR POST FOR THE PURPOSE OF MAKING A TREATY...

WHEN THEY GET THERE, KILL ALL THE GROWN INDIANS AND TAKE THE CHILDREN PRISONERS. THEN SELL THEM TO DEFRAY THE EXPENSE OF THE KILLING.

IN DUE TIME A COPY OF THIS ORDER REACHED JEFFERSON DAVIS, THE PRESIDENT OF THE CONFEDERACY.

DAVIS QUICKLY FIRED BAYLOR.

MR. BAYLOR REEMERGED AS A CONFEDERATE CONGRESSMAN FROM 1863 UNTIL THE END OF THE CIVIL WAR.

HE DIED IN MONTELL, TX IN 1894.

EMPEROR FERDINAND

JOSEPH MAXIMILIAN OF MEXICO (RIGHT FOREGROUND) WAS ABOUT TO BE OVERTHROWN IN 1867, SO HE DECIDED TO TAKE THE COUNTRY'S WEALTH WITH HIM. HE CHOSE 4 TRUSTED AUSTRIAN OFFICERS AND ABOUT 15 OR 20 LOYAL PEONS TO LOAD $10 MILLION WORTH OF GOLD, SILVER, AND JEWELS ON ABOUT 15 WAGONS.

TO AVOID AROUSING SUSPICION BY LOADING THE LOOT ON A SHIP IN A MEXICAN PORT, THE AUSTRIANS PLANNED A ROUNDABOUT ROUTE TO GALVESTON, TEXAS. AFTER MANY DAYS, THEY CROSSED THE RIO GRANDE AND MADE CAMP AT PRESIDIO DEL NORTE. HERE, 6 CONFEDERATE VETERANS FROM MISSOURI WANDERED INTO THE CAMP AND BEFRIENDED THE AUSTRIANS.

The Not-So-Friendly Escort

FOUR AUSTRIAN OFFICERS WERE SECRETLY TAKING MAXIMILIAN'S HORDE OF MEXICAN TREASURE ACROSS TEXAS TO A SHIP IN GALVESTON WHEN THEY MET 6 EX-CONFEDERATE SOLDIERS IN PRESIDIO COUNTY. WORRIED ABOUT OUTLAWS AND HOSTILE INDIANS, AND WITHOUT REVEALING THEIR CARGO, THE OFFICERS ASKED THEIR NEW FRIENDS TO ESCORT THEM AS FAR AS INDIANOLA.

THE GROUP REACHED CASTLE GAP, JUST EAST OF PRESENT-DAY ROUTE 385 AT THE BORDER OF CRANE & UPTON COUNTIES. HERE, THE CIVIL WAR VETS FOUND OUT ABOUT THE CONTENTS OF THE WAGONS AND KILLED THE AUSTRIANS AND ALL THE MEXICAN DRIVERS.

The Cache At Castle Gap

AFTER KILLING THE AUSTRIAN GUARDS AND MEXICAN DRIVERS, THE 6 EX-CONFEDERATE SOLDIERS BURIED MAXIMILIAN'S TREASURE AT CASTLE GAP. THEY CUT THE ANIMALS LOOSE AND BURNED THE WAGONS OVER THE BURIAL SITE. THEY FILLED THEIR POCKETS WITH ENOUGH LOOT TO MEET EXPENSES UNTIL THEY COULD RETURN, THEN SET OUT FOR SAN ANTONIO.

AT FORT CONCHO ONE OF THE MEN BECAME ILL. THE OTHERS DECIDED TO CONTINUE ON WITHOUT HIM.

BEFORE HE WAS FULLY RECOVERED, THE MAN SET OUT TO CATCH UP WITH HIS BUDDIES. HE FOUND THEIR BODIES ALONG THE TRAIL; THEY HAD BEEN KILLED BY HOSTILE INDIANS.

ONLY ONE MAN SURVIVED WHO KNEW THE LOCATION OF

Maximilian's Treasure,

BUT HE WAS VERY SICK AND DECIDED TO GO HOME TO MISSOURI.
ONE EVENING HE CAMPED WITH SOME MEN WHO HAPPENED TO BE
WANTED HORSE THIEVES. DURING THE NIGHT A POSSE CAPTURED
THE GANG AND PUT THEM IN JAIL IN DENTON, THE MISSOURIAN
WITH THEM.

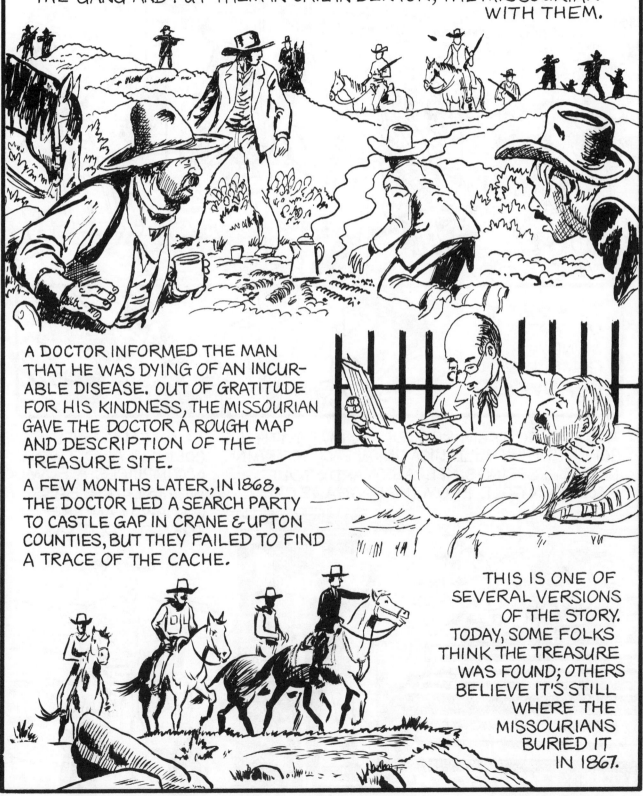

A DOCTOR INFORMED THE MAN
THAT HE WAS DYING OF AN INCUR-
ABLE DISEASE. OUT OF GRATITUDE
FOR HIS KINDNESS, THE MISSOURIAN
GAVE THE DOCTOR A ROUGH MAP
AND DESCRIPTION OF THE
TREASURE SITE.

A FEW MONTHS LATER, IN 1868,
THE DOCTOR LED A SEARCH PARTY
TO CASTLE GAP IN CRANE & UPTON
COUNTIES, BUT THEY FAILED TO FIND
A TRACE OF THE CACHE.

THIS IS ONE OF
SEVERAL VERSIONS
OF THE STORY.
TODAY, SOME FOLKS
THINK THE TREASURE
WAS FOUND; OTHERS
BELIEVE IT'S STILL
WHERE THE
MISSOURIANS
BURIED IT
IN 1867.

ILLITERATE AND ORPHANED AT 13,

SAM BASS

LEFT INDIANA IN 1869 AT THE AGE OF 18 AND DRIFTED WEST. EVENTUALLY HE GOT A JOB AS A COWBOY IN **DENTON.**

IN 1875 BASS AND **JOEL COLLINS** TOOK A HERD TO KANSAS, COLLECTED THE MONEY DUE THE OWNERS, AND HEADED FOR THE **BLACK HILLS.**

THEY LOST **ALL** OF THAT MONEY GAMBLING IN **DEADWOOD...**

AND TOOK TO TRAIN ROBBERY. IN 1877, WITH 4 COHORTS THEY HELD UP A UNION PACIFIC TRAIN NEAR BIG SPRINGS, NEBRASKA AND STOLE $60,000 IN GOLD FROM THE BAGGAGE CAR.

LAWMEN KILLED COLLINS AND TWO **ACCOMPLICES** A FEW WEEKS LATER. BASS GOT AWAY AND RETURNED TO TEXAS.

THE SAM BASS GANG

ON OCT. 12, 1877, SAM BASS RETURNED TO DENTON. BRAGGING ABOUT THE MONEY HE ROBBED FROM TRAINS, HE ENTICED FRANK JACKSON AND HENRY UNDERWOOD TO JOIN HIS GANG.

THEY PULLED THEIR FIRST JOB ON DEC. 20, 1877, HOLDING UP THE FORT WORTH–CLEBURNE STAGE. THEIR ENTIRE "TAKE" WAS $11.

ON CHRISTMAS DAY, SHERIFF EVERHART OF GRAYSON COUNTY MISTOOK UNDERWOOD FOR ANOTHER OUTLAW AND ARRESTED HIM AT HIS HOUSE.

The Unluckiest Gang in the West

HENRY UNDERWOOD, A MEMBER OF THE SAM BASS GANG WAS SENT TO JAIL IN NEBRASKA IN DECEMBER, 1877. THE ONLY ONES LEFT IN THE GANG WERE BASS AND FRANK JACKSON. ON FEB. 15, 1878 THEY ROBBED THE FORT WORTH-WEATHERFORD STAGE.

EACH GOT AWAY WITH $35 AND A WATCH.

SEABORN "SEBE" BARNES THREW IN WITH THEM. BASS ALSO RECRUITED TOM SPOTTSWOOD. NEXT, THE GANG HELD UP THE HOUSTON & TEXAS CENTRAL TRAIN AT ALLEN STATION, COLLIN COUNTY. IT WAS THE GANG'S BIGGEST SCORE. EACH OF THE FOUR NETTED $320.

SPOTTSWOOD WENT HOME AND WAS IMMEDIATELY ARRESTED. BASS AND THE OTHERS WERE NOT EVEN SUSPECTED.

No Way To Make a Living

HENRY UNDERWOOD REJOINED THE SAM BASS GANG IN MARCH, 1878 NEAR DENTON. HE HAD BROKEN OUT OF JAIL IN NEBRASKA AND BROUGT ALONG ANOTHER FUGITIVE NAMED "ARKANSAW JOHNSON."

ON APR.15, 1878 BASS PULLED HIS LAST ROBBERY, THAT OF THE TEXAS AND PACIFIC TRAIN AT MESQUITE. HIS "REGULARS" WERE THERE: BARNES, UNDERWOOD, JACKSON, & "JOHNSON," PLUS NINE OTHERS. THEY GOT $150, LEAVING EACH BANDIT A SHARE OF $10.71.

THE SAM BASS GANG OPERATED FROM DEC. 20, 1877 TO APR. 15, 1878. THEY MADE SIX HOLDUPS FOR A TOTAL "TAKE" OF $1,961. SINCE SAM ALWAYS TOOK AN EVEN SHARE, HE RECEIVED FOR SEVEN MONTHS' "WORK" A GRAND TOTAL OF $514.87.

A Special Company of Texas Rangers

UNDER MAJOR JOHN B. JONES WAS FORMED IN THE SPRING OF 1878 TO CAPTURE **SAM BASS** AND HIS **GANG**.

ONE NIGHT THEY SURPRISED A FEW OF BASS' MEN AT VALE CREEK IN WISE COUNTY. "ARKANSAW" JOHNSON WAS KILLED. HENRY UNDERWOOD FLED AND WAS NEVER SEEN AGAIN. JIM MURPHY OF DENTON WAS CAPTURED.

MURPHY WAS A COUSIN OF FRANK JACKSON, SAM BASS' RIGHT-HAND MAN. MAJOR JONES OFFERED TO LET MURPHY GO IF HE WENT BACK TO BASS AS AN INFORMANT FOR THE RANGERS. MURPHY AGREED.

BASS AND HIS GANG DECIDED TO LEAVE DENTON AND TRY FOR MEXICO. THEY PLANNED TO FINANCE THE TRIP BY ROBBING BANKS ALONG THE WAY.

Jim Murphy, the Snitch,

TALKED SAM BASS OUT OF ROBBING A BANK IN WACO AS THE BASS GANG WAS ENROUTE TO MEXICO. MURPHY DID THAT BECAUSE HE HAD NO TIME TO WARN MAJOR JONES SO THE TEXAS RANGERS COULD SET UP AN AMBUSH.

ON JULY 18, 1878, AT BELTON, MURPHY HURRIEDLY SCRAWLED A NOTE TO JONES: *"WE ARE ON OUR WAY TO* **ROUND ROCK** *TO ROB THE BANK. FOR GOD'S SAKE, PREVENT IT!"*

JONES IMMEDIATELY ORDERED LT. N.O. REYNOLDS AND 9 MORE RANGERS TO RUSH FROM THEIR CAMP AT SAN SABA, 75 MILES TO ROUND ROCK.

MEANWHILE, JONES AND OTHER RANGERS CONVERGED ON ROUND ROCK FROM AUSTIN. THE TRAP WAS SET.

30

Shoot-Out At Round Rock

SAM BASS HAD PLANNED TO ROB THE BANK IN ROUND ROCK ON SATURDAY, JULY 20, 1878. JIM MURPHY, THE INFORMANT, LAGGED BEHIND ON FRIDAY NIGHT WHEN THE GANG RODE INTO TOWN TO CASE THE JOINT. A POSSE OF TEXAS RANGERS, SHERIFFS, & DEPUTIES WERE WAITING...

BASS, "SEBE" BARNES, AND FRANK JACKSON ENTERED COPPREL'S STORE. DEPUTY SHERIFF GRIMES OF WILLIAMSON COUNTY & DEPUTY MAURICE MOORE WENT IN AFTER THEM. JACKSON AND BARNES OPENED FIRE, KILLING GRIMES. BASS WOUNDED MOORE.

THE BANDITS RAN FOR THEIR HORSES. DICK WARE, A TEXAS RANGER, RAN OUT OF A BARBER SHOP, SHOT BARNES AND WOUNDED BASS IN THE RIGHT HIP.

BASS AND JACKSON MANAGED TO ESCAPE.

The End Of The Line

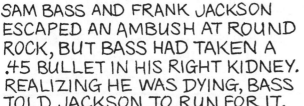

SAM BASS AND FRANK JACKSON ESCAPED AN AMBUSH AT ROUND ROCK, BUT BASS HAD TAKEN A .45 BULLET IN HIS RIGHT KIDNEY. REALIZING HE WAS DYING, BASS TOLD JACKSON TO RUN FOR IT.

THE NEXT MORNING, CPT. JAMES GILLETT, A RANGER FROM MARFA, FOUND BASS BARELY ALIVE UNDER AN OAK TREE.

THE RANGERS CARRIED SAM TO AN EMPTY SCHOOL WHERE HE DIED THE NEXT DAY, JULY 21, 1878. IT WAS HIS 27th BIRTHDAY. SAM BASS WAS BURIED IN THE *OLD* ROUND ROCK CEMETERY.

JIM MURPHY, THE INFORMANT, RETURNED HOME TO DENTON. NOBODY LIKED HIM. IT IS SAID HE DIED AFTER DRINKING A POISONOUS EYE WASH.

ACCORDING TO HIS DESCENDANTS, FRANK JACKSON WENT TO NEW MEXICO, CHANGED HIS NAME, GOT MARRIED & RAISED A FINE FAMILY.

Oran Milo Roberts

HAD BEEN A LAWYER AND DISTRICT ATTORNEY IN SAN AUGUSTINE DURING THE 1840's. IN 1857 HE BECAME A JUSTICE OF THE TEXAS **SUPREME COURT.**

AS THE COUNTRY TEETERED ON THE EDGE OF THE CIVIL WAR ROBERTS PRESIDED OVER THE SECESSIONIST CONVENTION IN JANUARY, 1861. CONSEQUENTLY, TEXAS JOINED THE **CONFEDERACY.**

EARLY IN 1862 HE RAISED A REGIMENT OF THE 11th TEXAS INFANTRY & SERVED AS ITS **COLONEL** UNTIL 1864.

THE TEXAS LEGISLATURE ELECTED ROBERTS AND DAVID G. **BURNETT** TO THE U.S. SENATE IN 1866, BUT THE YANKEES IN WASHINGTON REFUSED TO SEAT THEM BECAUSE TEXAS NEEDED MORE "RECONSTRUCTION."

The Gubernatorial Deadlock

THE STATE DEMOCRATIC CONVENTION OF 1878 IN AUSTIN WAS DEADLOCKED OVER PICKING A NOMINEE FOR GOVERNOR. FINALLY, THEY FORMED A COMMITTEE OF 32 DELEGATES WHO WOULD SELECT THEIR FAVORITES AMONG THE LEADING MEN OF THE STATE.

JUDGE ORAN MILO ROBERTS RECEIVED A MAJORITY OF 18 VOTES. HE WAS ON A FARM NEAR **TYLER** WHEN HE GOT THE NEWS.

ROBERTS IMMEDIATELY RODE INTO TOWN, BUT...

HE FORGOT HIS WALLET AND HAD TO BORROW "FOUR BITS" FROM A BARTENDER TO WIRE HIS ACCEPTANCE TO THE CONVENTION.

The Pardoning Governor

JUDGE ORAN ROBERTS BECAME GOVERNOR IN 1879 WHEN THE STATE WAS MIRED IN DEBT. TO REDUCE THE TAB, HE STARTED A "PAY AS YOU GO" PROGRAM, LOWERED PENSIONS, AND CUT BACK FUNDS FOR PUBLIC SCHOOLS.

HE STOPPED PAYING REWARDS FOR THE ARREST OF OUTLAWS AND, BY A LIBERAL POLICY OF PARDONS, RELIEVED THE CROWDED PRISONS.

A FRIEND TOLD ROBERTS THAT THE NEWSPAPERS AND CITIZENS WERE SAYING THAT TEXAS WAS GOING TO HELL UNDER THE USE OF HIS PARDONING POWER.

THE FORMER JUDGE REPLIED,

IF THE STATE GOES TO HELL UNDER MY RULE, IT WILL GO ACCORDING TO LAW!

SABINE COUNTY

GENEVA
HEMPHILL
PINELAND

WAS ORGANIZED ON DECEMBER 14, 1837.

THE AREA BECAME THE GATEWAY TO TEXAS FROM LOUISIANA WHEN MICHAEL CROW BEGAN TO RUN A FERRY ACROSS THE SABINE RIVER IN 1797. JAMES GAINES ESTABLISHED A LARGER FERRY A FEW MILES DOWNSTREAM IN 1812. HIS PASSENGERS INCLUDE FREEBOOTERS, FILIBUSTERS, SPIES, SOLDIERS AND SETTLERS.

AFTER THE CIVIL WAR, LUMBERING BECAME THE COUNTY'S MAIN INDUSTRY. THE FOREST WAS VIRTUALLY GONE BY 1920, AND THE TREND TURNED TOWARD CONSERVATION. THE U.S. FOREST SERVICE ACQUIRED ONE-THIRD OF THE COUNTY IN 1934 AND CREATED THE SABINE NATIONAL FOREST.

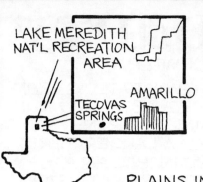

LAKE MEREDITH NAT'L RECREATION AREA

AMARILLO

TECOVAS SPRINGS

Potter County

WAS CREATED IN 1876 AND NAMED AFTER ROBERT POTTER, AN OFFICER IN THE TEXAS NAVY AND CONGRESSMAN IN THE TEXAS REPUBLIC.

PLAINS INDIANS, CONQUISTADORS, COMANCHEROS, PASTORES, TRADERS, AND MEXICAN SHEPHERDS CAMPED AT TECOVAS SPRINGS. IN 1881 THIS AREA BECAME THE HEADQUARTERS OF THE FRYING PAN RANCH, STARTED BY J.F. GLIDDEN AND HENRY SANBORN.

IN 1887 A RAILROAD CONSTRUCTION CAMP GREW OVERNIGHT INTO A TENT AND BUFFALO HUT SETTLEMENT CALLED *RAGTOWN*. WHEN THE COUNTY WAS ORGANIZED LATER THAT YEAR, *RAGTOWN* WAS COMBINED WITH ANOTHER CAMP, *ONEIDA*, TO BECOME AMARILLO, THE COUNTY SEAT.

Terrell County

WAS ORGANIZED IN 1905 AND NAMED IN HONOR OF ALEXANDER WATKINS TERRELL, AN AUSTIN POLITICIAN AND LT. COLONEL IN THE 34th TEXAS REGIMENT DURING THE CIVIL WAR.

SANDERSON

DRYDEN

RIO GRANDE

SANDERSON IS THE COUNTY SEAT. DURING THE LATE 1800's IT WAS A WILD FRONTIER TOWN, FREQUENTED BY GUNSLINGERS, CATTLE RUSTLERS, GOLD SEEKERS, AND BANDITS.

Charles Wilson's OLD COTTAGE BAR

ROY BEAN RAN A SALOON IN THE VILLAGE.

WILLIAM JESSE McDONALD WAS A TEXAS RANGER WITH A LIGHTNING-FAST DRAW, BUT HE USED IT ONLY TO DISARM. ONCE, HE BACKED DOWN BAT MASTERSON IN SANDERSON.

Bringing Culture to Northeast Texas

ITALIAN-BORN ANTHONY GHIO RAN A MERCANTILE STORE IN JEFFERSON FROM 1867 TO 1873. WHEN THE RESIDENTS REFUSED TO ALLOW JAY GOULD TO BUILD A RAILROAD THROUGH THE TOWN, GHIO MOVED TO TEXARKANA.

THERE, HE ORGANIZED A CATHOLIC CHURCH AND PROMOTED PAROCHIAL EDUCATION. HE BUILT AN OPERA HOUSE, AN ARTIFICIAL GAS PLANT, AND BROUGHT THE FIRST RAILROAD INTO THAT AREA.

HE OPENED A SECOND THEATER IN 1884 WITH A PERFORMANCE OF GILBERT & SULLIVAN'S "IOLANTHE." THREE YEARS LATER HE OPENED SPRING LAKE PARK.

MR. GHIO SERVED THREE TERMS AS MAYOR OF TEXARKANA. HE AND HIS WIFE HAD EIGHT CHILDREN. THEIR GRANDDAUGHTER, CORRINE GRIFFITH-MARSHALL WAS ONE OF THE FIRST SILENT SCREEN STARS.

SAM MARDOCK

WAS BORN 1863 IN CANTON, CHINA WITH THE NAME *MAR DOCK*. HE CAME TO TEXAS AS A RAILROAD EMPLOYEE IN 1880 AND WORKED AS AN INTERPRETER IN EL PASO AND GALVESTON.

HE OPENED A RESTAURANT IN TYLER IN 1890. IT WAS SO SUCCESSFUL THAT HE STARTED A CHAIN OF RESTAURANTS IN TOWNS SUCH AS LONGVIEW, KILGORE, AND GLADEWATER.

SAM BECAME KNOWN FOR HIS PHILANTHROPIES, AT ONE TIME DONATING LAND TO THE CITY OF TYLER FOR THE BECKHAM POPLAR OVERPASS.

MR. MARDOCK'S SONS, SAM AND JULIAN, WERE PILOTS IN WORLD WAR II. JULIAN (LEFT) WAS PROBABLY THE FIRST CHINESE-AMERICAN PILOT IN THE HISTORY OF MILITARY AVIATION.

The Belle of Tascosa

NOBODY EVER KNEW HER REAL NAME OR AGE. SHE WAS BORN IN LOUISIANA TO CREOLE PARENTS, SO FOLKS CALLED HER "FRENCHY." IN 1881 SHE TURNED UP IN THE WILD PANHANDLE TOWN OF TASCOSA AND MARRIED MICKEY McCORMICK, OWNER OF A SALOON AND GAMBLING JOINT. THEY CATERED TO SUCH NOTABLES AS BILLY THE KID, PAT GARRETT, BAT MASTERSON, AND CHARLES SIRINGO.

TASCOSA DECLINED AFTER THE RAILROAD BYPASSED IT IN 1897. THE McCORMICKS LOST THEIR BUSINESS, BUT CONTINUED TO LIVE IN THEIR ADOBE HOME. MICKEY DIED IN 1908.

BY 1915 THE TOWN WAS DESERTED, BUT "FRENCHY" LIVED THERE UNTIL 1939. SHE DIED IN 1941.

"IKE'S" BIRTHPLACE

ON OCTOBER 14, 1890, **DWIGHT DAVID EISENHOWER,** FUTURE FIVE-STAR GENERAL AND PRESIDENT OF THE UNITED STATES (1953-1961), WAS BORN IN THIS MODEST HOUSE IN **DENISON.** THE EISENHOWERS LIVED HERE WHILE THE FATHER WORKED FOR THE RAILROAD, BUT MOVED TO ABILENE, KANSAS SHORTLY AFTER DWIGHT DAVID WAS BORN. "IKE," AS HE WAS NICKNAMED, HAD NOT KNOWN ABOUT THIS HOUSE; HE THOUGHT HE WAS BORN IN TYLER UNTIL...

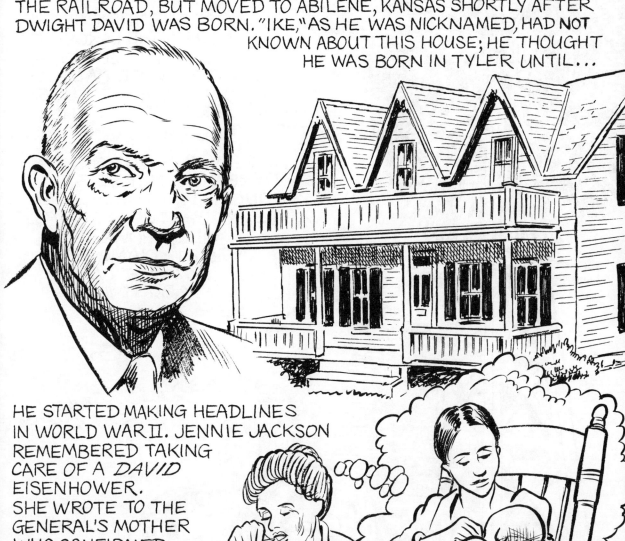

HE STARTED MAKING HEADLINES IN WORLD WAR II. JENNIE JACKSON REMEMBERED TAKING CARE OF A *DAVID* EISENHOWER. SHE WROTE TO THE GENERAL'S MOTHER WHO CONFIRMED THAT HER SON, DWIGHT DAVID WAS BORN IN DENISON.

IN 1953, A GROUP OF CITIZENS PURCHASED THE HOUSE. IT'S NOW A STATE HISTORIC SITE.

WINDMILLS

OPENED THE TEXAS PLAINS TO FARMERS, RANCHERS, & SETTLERS BY PUMPING WATER FROM VAST UNDERGROUND ROCK FORMATIONS.

AT THE TURN OF THE CENTURY, THE LARGE-SIZE WINDMILLS (16 TO 30 FT. IN DIAMETER) WERE CALLED "RAILROAD MILLS" BECAUSE MANY WERE USED TO PUMP WATER FOR STEAM LOCOMOTIVES.

BETWEEN 1905 AND 1914, FAIRBANKS, MORSE & CO. PRODUCED WHAT IT CALLED A "TEXAS PATTERN" *ECLIPSE* MILL, SHOWN HERE. A **25** FT.-DIAMETER *ECLIPSE* COST ABOUT $300.

TODAY, THE LARGEST OPERATIONAL WINDMILL IN THE UNITED STATES IS ON THE **CANON RANCH** IN WESTERN PECOS COUNTY.

Echols' Silver Scam

NOBODY KNEW THAT A MAN CALLING HIMSELF JUNE ECHOLS WAS A CON ARTIST WHEN, IN 1900, HE RODE INTO STONEWALL COUNTY AND PURCHASED SOME LAND IN JONES CANYON.

HE LAID OUT A TOWN CALLED ORIENT. TO ATTRACT INVESTORS HE ANNOUNCED THAT HE DISCOVERED SILVER AND OPENED A MINE.

HUNDREDS RUSHED TO BUY TOWN LOTS AND SHARES IN THE MINE. WITHIN WEEKS ORIENT HAD 200 TENTS AND A POPULATION OF A FEW THOUSAND.

BY THE TIME THE INVESTORS REALIZED THAT ECHOLS "PLANTED" THE SILVER IN THE MINE, HE HAD VANISHED.

The First Intercity Bus Service

IN TEXAS BEGAN OPERATING BETWEEN COLORADO CITY AND SNYDER ON OCTOBER 29, 1907. THE VEHICLE, ONE OF THE FIRST COMMERCIALLY DESIGNED MOTORBUSES IN THE COUNTRY, WAS HAND-BUILT BY THE WESTERN MOTOR CO. OF LOGANSPORT, INDIANA AT A COST OF $735. IT HAD NO MUFFLER.

THERE WERE NO ROADS BETWEEN THE TWO TOWNS AND THAT FIRST BUS TO SNYDER ARRIVED LATE BECAUSE IT WAS STUCK IN A DITCH FOR A FEW HOURS. THEREAFTER BUSINESS PROSPERED UNTIL...

THE CITIZENS TOLD THE OWNER, W.B. CHENOWETH TO TAKE HIS NOISY MACHINE ELSEWHERE. HE MOVED TO BIG SPRING AND STARTED A BUS SERVICE FROM THERE TO LAMESA. THE 55-MILE TRIP TOOK 8 OR 9 HOURS.

Eddie Rickenbacker, Car Salesman

IN 1909, FIFE & MILLER, A DALLAS CAR DEALER, COMPLAINED THAT THEIR FIRESTONE-COLUMBUS AUTOMOBILES KEPT BREAKING DOWN. THE OHIO-BASED MANUFACTURER SENT AN 18 YEAR-OLD MECHANIC TO FIX THEM. HIS NAME WAS EDDIE RICKENBACKER. HE ALTERED THE ENGINES TO TOLERATE THE TEXAS HEAT.

RICKENBACKER HELPED START CAR DEALERSHIPS ALL OVER TEXAS. AS A PUBLICITY STUNT HE CHAUFFEURED PRESIDENTIAL CANDIDATE WILLIAM JENNINGS BRYAN (BACK SEAT-LEFT) THROUGH ABILENE.

NINE YEARS LATER, DURING WORLD WAR I, RICKENBACKER WAS GEN. BILLY MITCHELL'S DRIVER, THEN BECAME AMERICA'S LEADING FIGHTER PILOT. HE SHOT DOWN 26 GERMAN AIRPLANES AND WON THE CONGRESSIONAL MEDAL OF HONOR.

The Father Of Texas Folklore

J. FRANK DOBIE QUIT HIS $100 A MONTH JOB AS A UNIVERSITY OF TEXAS ENGLISH INSTRUCTOR IN 1920 AND WENT TO WORK AT HIS UNCLE'S CATTLE RANCH. EVERY EVENING A COWBOY NAMED SANTOS CORTEZ TOLD FOLKTALES. THIS GAVE DOBIE THE IDEA TO COLLECT AND PRESERVE THE LEGENDARY TALES OF TEXAS.

THE BOTTOM DROPPED OUT OF THE CATTLE MARKET AND DOBIE WENT BACK TO THE UNIVERSITY IN 1921 AND BECAME TEXAS' FIRST GREAT LITERARY FIGURE. HE PRESERVED THOUSANDS OF TEXAS TALES AND MEMOIRS THAT WOULD HAVE DIED WITH THEIR TELLERS. HE WROTE 25 BOOKS; MOST ARE STILL IN PRINT. HE ALSO HELPED FOUND THE TEXAS FOLKLORE SOCIETY.

PECANS

WHILE CABEZA de VACA WAS A PRISONER OF THE INDIANS IN THE EARLY 1530's, THEY TOOK HIM TO THE "RIVER OF MANY NUTS," NOW THE GUADALUPE. THERE, THE INDIANS GORGED THEM- SELVES WITH PECANS. WHEN CABEZA ESCAPED TO MEXICO, HE TOOK PECANS WITH HIM.

TODAY, TEXAS IS THE LEADING PECAN STATE, PRODUCING ABOUT 30% OF THE NATION'S CROP. NO WONDER IT IS THE STATE TREE.

THIS DRAWING OF A PECAN TREE SHAKER WAS MADE AT THE IRISH ACRES PECAN PLANTATION NEAR LUBBOCK.

Tent Show Vaudeville

HARLEY SADLER GREW UP IN STAMFORD, TEXAS, AND LEFT HOME AT 17 TO JOIN THE PARKER BROTHERS CARNIVAL. OVER THE NEXT FEW YEARS HE WAS AN ACTOR WITH SEVERAL TRAVELING VAUDEVILLE COMPANIES.

IN 1914, AT THE AGE OF 22, SADLER BECAME THE SECOND BANANA (COMEDIAN) FOR THE ROY E. FOX PLAYERS, AN ELABORATE TRAVELING TENT SHOW. THIS WAS WHERE HE DEVELOPED HIS "CRAZY COWBOY" ROUTINE.

WHEN HARLEY BOUGHT HIS OWN SHOW IN 1922, IT BECAME ONE OF THE MOST POPULAR VAUDEVILLE TENT SHOWS IN THE SOUTHWEST. FOR A QUARTER CENTURY IT PLAYED ANNUALLY IN 60 TOWNS IN WEST TEXAS AND NEW MEXICO. MR. SADLER SUFFERED A FATAL HEART ATTACK IN 1954 WHILE EMCEEING A BENEFIT FOR THE BOY SCOUTS IN AVOCA.

The First Television Station In Texas

WAS WBAP-TV, OWNED BY THE *FORT WORTH STAR-TELEGRAM.* THEY FILED FOR A PERMIT WITH THE FCC IN 1946 AND WENT ON THE AIR TWO YEARS LATER. THEIR FIRST PROGRAM WAS PRESIDENT HARRY TRUMAN'S "WHISTLE STOP" AT THE T&P TERMINAL IN FORT WORTH, SEPT. 27, 1948. FRANK MILLS WAS THE ANNOUNCER.

TWO DAYS LATER, WBAP-TV CHANNEL FIVE TELECAST ITS FIRST LIVE SHOW FEATURING THE FLYING X RANCH BOYS.

LONDON HAS "BIG BEN," BUT **CLARKSVILLE**, TEXAS HAS

"BIG RED."

THE TOWER CLOCK ON THE **RED RIVER COUNTY** COURTHOUSE, KNOWN AS "BIG RED," WAS INSTALLED IN 1885 AND RAN CONTINUOUSLY UNTIL 1961, WHEN IT WAS CONVERTED TO ELECTRICITY.

THE $1,750 CLOCK DID NOT LIKE THE CHANGE AND REBELLED BY **RINGING** ITS 2,000-LB. BELL **120 TIMES** BEFORE SOMEONE PULLED THE PLUG.

When the Yanks Became the Texans

THE NEW YORK YANKS WAS A NATIONAL FOOTBALL LEAGUE FRANCHISE OWNED BY ENTERTAINER TED COLLINS. FINANCIAL TROUBLES FORCED HIM TO SELL THE TEAM BACK TO THE **NFL** IN JANUARY, 1952 FOR $100,000.

THE LEAGUE, IN TURN, SOLD THE YANKS TO GILES MILLER, OWNER OF TEXTILE MILLS IN DALLAS. THIS BECAME THE FIRST NFL TEAM IN THE SOUTH: THE **DALLAS TEXANS.**

THE TEXANS FARED NO BETTER THAN THEY DID AS THE YANKS. BY THEIR FIRST MID-SEASON, THEY HAD LOST OVER A QUARTER MILLION DOLLARS AND MOST OF THEIR GAMES.

ON NOVEMBER 12, 1952, MILLER RETURNED THE FRANCHISE TO THE NFL. THE TEXANS PLAYED OUT THE SEASON AS A "ROAD CLUB" OPERATED BY THE LEAGUE.

AT THE TIME, TOM LANDRY WAS A LEFT HALFBACK WITH THE NY GIANTS.

About the Author - Artist

Patrick M. Reynolds researches, writes, illustrates, and syndicates two state historical cartoons every week: *Pennsylvania Profiles* and *Texas Lore,* and one on New York City called *Big Apple Almanac.* Patrick attended Minersville (PA) High School, Pratt Institute, Brooklyn, NY, and earned a Masters of Fine Arts degree in Illustration at Syracuse (NY) University.

Lt. Col. Reynolds is a veteran of the Vietnam War and a member of the US Army Reserves. Patrick and his wife, Patricia, live in the Lancaster County, Pennsylvania town of Willow Street with their two daughters, Kimberly Jo and Maria Alyssa, and their son, Thomas Patrick.

Below is a sample of Mr. Reynolds' Pennsylvania feature.

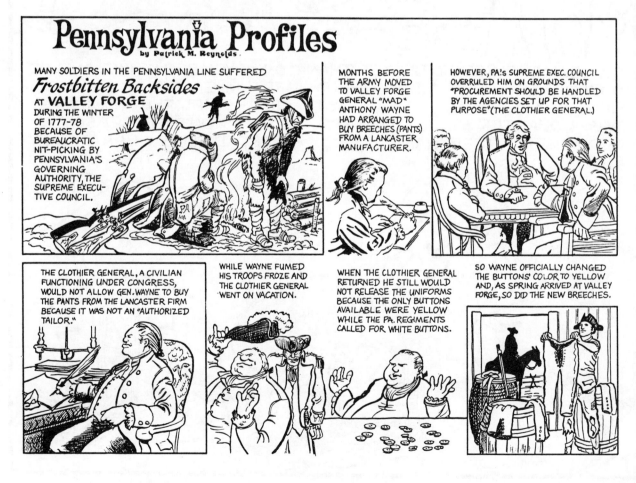